Bein a Strong Black Woman
Can Get U Killed!!

To Selina;

Peace, Love 'n
Power.

Lauri

Bein a Strong Black Woman
Can Get U Killed!!

Laini Mataka

Bein A Strong Black Woman Can Get U Killed

A DuForcelf book published by Black Classic Press
2000
All Rights Reserved
Library of Congress Catalog Card No. TBA
ISBN 1–57478–002–6

Printed by BCP Digital Printing, a division of Black Classic Press

Founded in 1978, Black Classic Press specializes in bringing to light obscure and significant works by and about people of African descent. If our books are not available in your area, ask your local bookseller to order them. Our current list of titles can be obtained by writing:

Black Classic Press
c/o List
P.O. Box 13414
Baltimore, MD 21203

A Young Press With Some Very Old Ideas

THIS BOOK IS DEDICATED TO MY ANCESTORS: The Queen Esther, Ellen Garvin, Lawrence Garvin, Aunt Sebee, Uncle Guy, Victoria, Ethel, Lawrence, Ruth, JC, Leroy, Elln, Sara, Louise, Lessie, Uncle Sidney, Sidney Jr., Ernest, Liza Robinson, Monroe Robinson, Malcolm, Uncle Theodore, Uncle Alfred, Aunt Maude, Aunt Viola, Aunt Liola, Grandmotha Adele, Grandfatha David Howard, Cousin Roxanne, Uncle Freddie, Hortense, Arsell, Peggy, Big Walter and Inez, Loogie, Gerald, Robert, Teddy and Saundra, Cupid, Will Green, Freeda, Jackie, John Harvey, Vincent and Juanita Jones, Juanita Brown, Mil Butler, Raymond Etta and Chap, The Byrds, The Burnetts. ESPECIALLY: Mildred and Eugene Robinson, Arizander Robinson, Nez the Honorable John H. Clarke, Kenny Kirkland, Betty Carter, Ron Brown, James Byrd, Queen Mother Moore, Jimmy Grey

ILLNESS IS GOD'S WAY OF LETTING YOU KNOW WHO CARES. THANKS & MUCH LOVE TO: Kokaye, Mwangaza, Imani, Audri, Kimberly, Renee, Mike, Ako, Eisha, Sister Kay, JoAnn, Sadiqua, Johnny, Annette, Veroneca, Heru and Eleanor, Kevin and Regina, Trunita, Hermine, Rose, Vanessa, Sadiqua and Rock, Faye, Maria Guevara, Juma, Menes Angie, Selene, Debbie, Sean, Nadine, Mama Binta and family, Isisara, Kinya, Thaia, Dominque, Paul (as usual), Prem, Cheikh, Musa, SACRED SPACE, SISTERSPACE, YAWA, ADACI, MARTHA'S TABLE AND SOLDIER'S CORNER.

Table of Contents

BEIN A STRONG BLACK WOMAN
CAN GET U KILLED!

on April 25, 1997, at 11:55 pm
while strugglin with the reality of bein a human
instead of a myth, the strong blk woman passed away,
w/out the slightest bit of hoopla
medical sources say: she died from naturally oppressive causes
but those who knew her & used her / kno that she died from:
bein silent when she shldve been **screamin**
smilin when she shldve been ragin.
she died from bein sick & not wantin anyone
to kno / becuz her pain might inconvenience them.
she died from an overdose of otha people
clingin on to her when she didnt even have energy for herself.

she died from luvin men who didnt luv themselves
& cld only offer her a crippled reflection.
she died from raisin children alone & bein criticized for
not doin a complete job.
she died from the lies her grandmotha told her motha
          & her motha told her, about life, racism & men.
she died from bein sexually abused as a child
& havin to take that truth everywhere she went
every day of her life, exchangin the humiliation
for guilt & back again. she died from bein
battered by someone who claimed to luv her & she allowed
the batterin to go on to show / that she luvvvv'd him too.

she died from asphyxiation, coughin up blood
from secrets she kept tryin to burn away
instead of allowin herself the kind of nervous
break-down she was entitled to, **but only wite girls**

Being A Strong Black Woman

cld afford. she died from bein responsible,
becuz she was the last rung on the ladder & there
was no one under her she cld dump on.

  the strong blk woman is DEAD

she died from the multiple births of children she
never really wanted but was forced to have by the stranglin
morality of those around her.
she died from bein a motha at 15 & a grandmotha
at 30 & an ancestor at 45. she died from bein
dragged down & sat upon by un-evolved women posin
as sistahs. she died from pretendin the life she
was livin was a kodak moment instead of a 20th century
post-slavery nightmare.

she died from toleratin mr. pitiful, just to have
a man around the house. she died from lack of orgasms
becuz she never learned what made her body happy
& no one ever took the time to teach her.
& sometimes when she found arms that were tender,
she died, becuz they were the same gender.
she died from sacrificin herself for everybody &
everything when what she really wanted to do was
be a singer, a dancer or some magnificent otha.

she died from lies of omission becuz she didnt
want to be accused of bringin the blkman down.
she died from race memories of bein snatched & raped
& snatched & sold & snatched & bred & snatched
& whipped & snatched & worked to death.

she died from tributes from her counterpart / who
shldve been matchin her efforts instead of showerin
her with dead words & empty songs. she died from

Can Get U Killed

myths that wldnt allow her to show weakness w/out
bein chastised by the   lazy & the hazy. she died from
hidin her real feelins until they became monstrously hard &
bitter enuff to invade her womb & breasts like angry tumors.
she died from **always liftin somethin** from heavy boxes
to refrigerators.

the strong blk woman is DEAD

she died from the punishments received from bein
honest about life, racism & men. she died from bein
called a bitch for bein verbal, a dyke for bein assertive
& a whore for pickin her own lovers.

she died from never bein enuff of what men wanted or bein
too much for the men she wanted. she died from bein too blk
& died again for not bein blk enuff.

she died from castration every time somebody thought of her
as only a woman, or treated her like less than a man.
she died from bein misinformed about her mind, her body
& the extent of her royal capabilities. she died
from knees pressed too close togetha becuz respect was
never a part of the foreplay that was bein shoved at her.
she died of loneliness in birthin rooms & aloneness in
abortion centers. she died of shock
in court-rooms where she sat, alone, watchin her children
legally lynched. she died in bathrooms with her veins
bustin open with **self-hatred & neglect.** she died in her mind,
fightin life, racism & men, while her body was carted away &
stashed in a human warehouse for the spiritually mutilated.

& sometimes, when she refused to die, when she just refused to
go out like that,

Being A Strong Black Woman

she was killed
>   by lethal images of blonde hair, blue eyes
>   & flat butts

rejected to death by the oj.'s, quincy's & poitier's.
sometimes, she was **stomped to death** by racism & sexism
executed by hi-tech ignorance
while she carried the family in her belly, the community on her
head, & the race on her back.

WELL, the STRONG, SILENT, SHIT-TAKIN blk woman is
officially **DEAD**.

Will the **real queens** please.....................**RISE!**

YR KISS

i spend too much time evaluating yr mouth
odd moments of the day find me caged
in the leathery softness of yr lips
wrestling with my nips.
yr mouth, even in sleep
is a luscious predator that entices me
out of starring in my own dreams,
to be a second-rate contender in yrs.

when i pull the sheet away from yr body
it's just so i can program my senses
to recognize the physical structure of fulfillment
which seems to culminate in the butterfly lips u use
to suck me into shock.

u make of my tongue a prisoner-of-war
that never wants to be liberated
with carefully maneuvered strokes
u leave me on the flame-tipped platform
of erotika's stargate.

nobody kisses me like u do.

nobody glorifies my mouth the way u do,
& i hold on to each kiss, until
yr absence PRIES my lips away.

the memory of kisses past
makes me shiver, til a river of lava
spurts out of the fountainhead of my
southern hemisphere.

Being A Strong Black Woman

here now, in hunger's ominous grasp
my mind twitches suspiciously
wondering where yr mouth is
& WHO
    is staring at it, wantingly.

ON BOTH SIDES OF TIME

on both sides of time, i've probed
sometimes, getting caught between the teeth of living memory
i've pushed centuries aside, keepin time at bay
so i cld perform the endless task of
trailing the remnants of yr smiles
as they trickle down thru the ages
imprisoning me in a time-capsuled affair
that thinks itself a holiday
deserving veneration
every night of every star-crossed day.

nail-clippings, a hint of musk, rose-petals
& a 19th century lock of yr hair
are all i have to show of a luv
that has been energized by death
freeze-dried, by unrelenting passion
& engraved in the stone of my being.

Being A Strong Black Woman

THE TURQUOISE SERIES

1

only people who
eat every
day, can af
ford to think abstract.

2

life is too high a
price to pay for
letting stran
gers,in yr chambers.

3

when u run out of
fruit, just pluck me
and let my
juices whip yr tongue.

TO MY BROTHAS IN BLOOD

i never ask anything of u
though a call, a card or a note
wld blow me delightfully away.

i never ask anything of u
not that u care for me or even think of me
i ask for nothing/becuz i'm afraid
of being given less than that.

i have always been there for u
the sistah nobody knew u had
the one that ustah be on the radio
the one that utah dance
the one that wrote books/that u
have never read or even inquired about.

i have always been shackled to u
the way u have always been shackled to that powder
i wish u needed my blackness like u need that whiteness
i wish u wld come to me like u go to yr dealer
he can only soothe u temporarily
i can give u a high that will never go away
& never kill u.

i have always been proud of u
loving the way u look/wishing i was as dark
loving the way our father favored u
while i was marked effeminate
& stored in the ice-box.

i have always needed u to protect me
play with me, argue with me, teach street

Being A Strong Black Woman

& male differences to me.
i have always wanted othas to kno that i had
back-up & that if they messed with me
i had brothas who wld come like marines
to invade their bodies with sistah-loving punches.

i have always needed u to acknowledge me
needed u to tell yr friends about me, needed u
to compare yr girl-friends to me, needed u
to include me as aunty in the lives of yr children.

i have always luv'd u
& always wondered if u ever thought of me
as anything otha than yr half-sistah,
who lives somewhere,
                down the way.

WHEN A LYNCHIN WAS LIKE A LUNCHEON
(for James Cameron & Zachariah Walker)

how many blk people have truly been lynched,
we, the un-lynched, will never kno.
& if like some, u are too afraid to contemplate the numbers
then u need to high-tail it away from this pome.
cuz this pome aint for chumps.
this pome aint for those still practicin denial over alllll
the atrocities committed against our precious species.
this pome aint for people who wanna forget
this pome aint for people who wanna leave the past in the past
this pome is for the physical, mental & spiritual warriors
dedicated to balancin the scales no matter how long it takes.

dare with me now, to wonder—how did it feel
to cut that strange fruit down?
how did it feel to see the inhabitants of yr heart, hangin
danglin from faultless trees, covered with flies, like rottin
fruit? how did it feel to see the somebody yr world was built
around swingin from an innocent branch, face smashed,
neck broken
private parts ripped off. how did the lovers of the dead
feel, havin to sneak onto the scene to steal away the bodies of
the beloved? how long did those bodies have to hang
before friends & family felt it safe enough to rescue their
shells?
how did it feel to know who the murderers were
& yet, not even be able to whisper their names in yr dreams?

how cripplin was the terror that spread from soul to soul?
how many layers of being were penetrated by the dread
of knowin it cld happen to anyone at any time?

Being A Strong Black Woman

did the dead have funerals, or were they smuggled
into the ground & hurried to their ancestors who cld offer them
more security than the living?
how long after the lynchins did it take before people dared
to walk down the road again at night? & when confronted
with the devils, what kind of deodorant was used to muffle
the scent of hatred pourin forth from the souls of the victims'
loved ones? & just how disguised was the revenge, & how many
blk families had to flee, after the deeds were done?

gil-scott posed the question & i aint heard an answer yet: "who'll
pay reparations for my soul?"
somebody's got to pay, or does payment come swaggerin
in nuances—a dead wite body, found somewhere, sometime mur-
dered by somebody, somewhere.
a denny williams on a righteous day, & the confused cries
of the amnesiatic multitudes who only wanna know why?

& how many times did our people ask the same mysterious
question? knowin no hystorikal reason for the
ever-grown malice, the seemingly innate ambivalence.
wonderin how long cld such times last.
wonderin if God was tryin to tell us something that we
lacked the courage to hear.

understand: DEAD WITE BODIES, murdered by blk hands
that u get no sympathy here. not after the many times
yr xenophobic ancestors sat around enjoyin picnics that
were organized around the deaths of the niggahs they had just
picked, to be beaten, castrated, & barbqued for a Sunday
afternoon's entertainment.
they were proud of the lynchins which were just like luncheons.
they took pictures of themselves standin next to the kill

Can Get U Killed

as if they were big-time game hunters
they smiled from the heart in those pictures
they were surrounded by their wives & children
whoopin it up as if they were all on holiday
they didnt even have to know the victim.
didnt have to have a beef with him
didnt even have to personally dislike him
it only mattered that he was their natural enemy
& whenever & wherever **it was their duty** to kill him
& in celebration of that belief
they ate heartily while the stench of a dead blk person's flesh
provided ambiance.

HELL NO, u get no sympathy here.
& i over-understand that random violence against wite people
aint really random. its in our blood
where memory cant be lobotomized, or bludgeoned to death
the price of righteousness is in the blood
& who knos what lynched ancestors possess the souls
of our young. maybe,
they're not as bazaar, beserk, & bewildered as they seem
maybe they listen with a part of themselves we're afraid
to acknowledge. maybe hiphop is their antennae, the internal
hearin device that connects them to some ancestors we havent
as of yet, recognized. maybe they seem crazy
cuz nobody ever taught them to identify the voices that rap in
their heads, invitin them to **seize the time.**

everybody's afraid of the new-jack city dwellers
they cant see the irony in the fact that we werent able to protect
our beloved, then. werent able to avenge them, once they were
dead. but there is irony here. nobody can protect wite people
from the descendants of the lynched.

Being A Strong Black Woman

that's why they be tryin to get into outer space
(which is also blk)
that's why they're tryin to hook up forever imprisonment for
those who've committed a violent crime for the 3rd time
cuz if u've had the guts to go ballistic 3 times,
aint nothin they can do to instill fear in u. the dayze
of consequence-free killin of blks is officially over & along with
the bubba's & the lil man's names in the obituaries
will also read the tods & the isaacs—cuz from now on
when we're forced to meet our maker, we aint goin
on that trip alone.

& what this pome is fighin to say, is that

it doesnt matter how i feel, whether i talk shit now
& run later or have a wite-out & lose my soul
RIGHTeousness, will be enacted
whether i participate or not, whether i condemn or condone
the balancin of the scales doesnt need my approval or yours
& if u're not gonna be an instrument of justice
just get the hell outa the way, cuz our blues has gone full circle

& we have debts to pay!

Can Get U Killed

GREAT EXPECTATIONS

i cldnt believe it.
he had **big** hands, **big** feet
he was 6' somethin
long, lean, elegant, & pointed,
& i cldnt believe it!

when we were dancin, i cldve sworn
abundance was nigh.
my senses must need glasses
& my power of touch needs to be drastically honed.

i aint one for believin
in the motion of the ocean/i'm concerned
about the size of the ship
cuz if all i'm workin with is a canoe
i might as well swim back to shore
by my damn self.

i just cldnt believe it!

after all the years of
languishin lovingly in the shadows of plenty
here i am, gaspin at scarcity
& tryin to come up with an erogenous way
to keep history from repeatin itself.

Being A Strong Black Woman

CELESTIAL BLUES

not to me, do angels speak or touch
with winged fervor.
my soul is lucky to catch the slightest shadow
of a revelation, or
even the coat-tail of a dream.

outside of my hearing
oracles make themselves known
they tango at the edge of my vision
& walk the highwire over the valley of my consciousness.

where i cannot see him, does my true luv exist
breathing w/out me
not even missing me in his fantasies.

which just goes to show, that too often
my moments lose their majik, somewhere
between heaven's apathy
& hell's indifference.

Can Get U Killed

ONCE YOU'VE BEEN THERE,
U CAN NEVER GO BACK

it's been over a year now, since he discovered
the spot it's not like he'd been lookin for it
or even knew it existed.

they were both bored, trapped in a glass ball of
ice & snow. & tired of doin all the distracting
things they cld think of, they decided to. . .

so they worked their way up the stairs
& had almost made it to the hall when he
sweet-mouthed her into an early opening
that cushioned his entry with a fluid eagerness
that wiped his mental faculties right out!

the pictures on the wall, were nothing
compared to their image on the wall, slipping & sliding
to the tune of a song their bodies sang
becuz their minds were embarrassed by the words.

something about the wall freed them from their
inhibitions—raw fucking sneaked up on them
made them clench their teeth, while distorted faces
begged for more & more. & somewhere between
the curses & the fireworks, he found **the spot** that made her
muscles freeze him into such an
orgasmically beautiful place, that his
libido flicked off all consciousness & with one
elegant thrust, painlessly split the core that
rocked her onto the floor & left them both
in a babbling aftershock of **"damn! what happened?"**

Being A Strong Black Woman

but that was a year ago. & since then, he's almost lost his mind
trying to explore the genital geography that will lead him back to
where she prays every night
that the gods will reveal
the spot.

SHOE-SHINE MAN

an amerikan anachronism
how dare u do—that which
embarrasses us, by remindin us
of jigaboo dayze long gone, except
in the white house.
the rhythms u cultivate
catch us stiff-legged
refusin to remember the tunes
that made us bleed yet saved our lives.

master of self-reliance
alternative life-style maker
with a box & some rags
u strive to make that which lacks lustre
shine.

some still think that yr head down
means they can lift theirs a bit higher
what they & on-lookers, fail to note
is that after all the spittin & waxin
buffin & glowin
it is **yr reflection**
that is perfected.

Being A Strong Black Woman

LICORICE

as a child, i hated licorice
didnt like the way it got all up in my teeth
w/out really bein sweet.
i never really thought of it as candy
til i licked yr fingers,
tongued the twisted length
of yr sunburnt legs.
i thought licorice was for kids,
till i tasted yr arms bindin me
shockin my taste-buds into expandin
& includin yr navel as a newly found delicacy.
hatin licorice the way i did
how was i to know
that between yr steel-plated thighs
the delectable grew
good & plenty
forcin me to feast w/out gettin fat
drink, w/out gettin drunk
yr ability to shift-shape into licorice
has been one of erotika's best kept secrets
& now, every time i see u
i feel like i'm in a candy-shop
measurin by the pound
& it's all i can do
to keep my tongue in my mouth.

Can Get U Killed

LAST NIGHT, I DID NOT DIE...

last night, i did not die by earthquake
       in japan.
broken glass did not fly into my future,
cutting the possibilities down to nothing.
the buildings i've spent my life entering
       did not
fall on me, or cancel my tomorrows.

last night, i did not die by earthquake
       in japan.
the ground did not open up & swallow my family
trees did not collapse on the faces of past lovers.
the wailing of children being crushed
did not pierce the serenity of my dreams.

last night, i did not die by earthquake
       in japan.
nature did not wreak havoc on my home
did not vent her frustration on my surroundings
did not assert her omnipotence at my humble expense.

last night, i did not die by earthquake
       in japan.
& this morning's total of the death & destruction
have me precariously balanced between shame & gratitude
       & i ask the victims' forgiveness
       becuz last night, **i slept well.**

TEMPLE VIOLATIONS

like somethin out of a book he had just read, he sd
i'm gonna change the way u feel about men
u cant just group them all togetha & say they aint...
i'm gonna turn yr world right-side up & make u testify.

so he laid me down, the way God must have laid down the earth
he stole words from my own mouth & used them
like esoteric keys to unlock doors I didnt even know I had.

he moved like a man who knew what he was doin
he sd, he wanted to restore the queen, between strokes
he sd he was givin me the tip of the iceberg
& plunged into me like a man on a mission
a funk-filled jihad
he waged war against all my notions of how good/good cld be
he touched my face with the lightness of a butterfly's wings
kissed my eyes with the subtlety of silk
he worked like a generator to pull me up out of myself
to bring my essence almost to the surface
just so he cld say he'd experienced it.

he worked me like a whore who knew
that befores & afters were far more crucial than
lickin & stickin.

he rock & rolled me, incited & ignited me
he just kept reachin into me, DEEPer & DEEPer
believin that gold had to be there.
& he was right, only he, apparently
was not accustomed to the maintenance of gold
only its **exploration.**

Can Get U Killed

i cld have died right there, grinding pelvises into dust,
in double-barreled syncopation
romance retreated somewhere, to redefine herself
& lust was like a soldier
determined to slay my inhibitions
& seduce the spirits that guarded my soul.

if he had been sincere
one nite of him cld have healed months of damage
my mind & heart had incurred.

if he had meant even half of what he claimed
i cld have gotten up the next mornin & told my last ten
grisly experiences, to go straight back to hell.

if he had meant any part of what he so theatrically did & sd
he cld have walked off into the dawn w/out
me tryin to hold him back, such wld have been my gratitude
that i wld have sacrificed my own desire
to be with him
for his desire to be with anotha.

but, when he sucked up the last of me as if i were a mango
he spit out the seed & walked away.
he clda planted that seed & grown the best friend
anybody cld ever want,
but he spit it out & snapped right back
into his body-countin world
& when i called, becuz it felt natural to wanna connect
with someone who a few days ago
had tied his being up into mine like the roots of a petrified tree
he had already forgotten my voice, & after pickin up on it
went on to talk like a stranger who had given someone

Being A Strong Black Woman

their number, just to be polite
but really hadnt expected or wanted them to call.

temple violations
shld be taken as seriously as murder
the way u enter, experience & exit someone's temple
can either imbue them with the honeysuckle profoundities of life
or leave them languishin
in the shadows of **seduction and abandonment.**

SEDUCING THE LIGHT FANTASTIK

fascinated by the glow of unabashed vulva lips
the kingman, with a poised mouth, seeks to ensnare
that glow with homespun flickers of unfed tongue
til her cries float effortlessly
on the crimson ripples of trojan-coated, pulsating lust.

standing at attention, his sensibilities culminate
in a quivering dance of head pointing towards delight.

a solar driven creature with a phd in carnalogy
her body crucifies his nerve-endings with
swift attacks of grinding strategies
that leave his body shocked
& his soul, exalted.

during one of the millenniums that passed between the days
they were reported missing
police & firemen were brought to the scene of the
alleged crime, but
even they cld not explain the burnt engravings on the
purple-satin sheets or offer one clue
as to the whereabouts of the absent lovers.

yet deep in the heart of a sleeping mali
two master-sky watchers of the Dogon
sat side by side silently rejoicing
at the appearance of two new stars
beaming down streams of ultra-satisfaction
throughout the erotik universe.

Being A Strong Black Woman

HAPPY BIRTHDAY MLK

amerikans are good
at keepin the dream alive
while killin its fulfillment.
if u came back tomorrow
they'd kill u
& stuff u
& place u
in the center of a hollow-caust museum
& charge us $10 a-piece
to come in & apologize.

THE SISTAHS RAN TOO
(For Linda Brent)

w/out taking time to do their hair, paint their nails
or match their colors, the sistahs ran.
they left men they luv'd to get away from men they hated
they left their mamas & sistahs & babies
in the care of people who werent allowed to
control any part of their existence.

they left everything they knew in exchange for a more
favorable position in the unknown.
they ran w/out pocketbooks, addresses to go to,
names to invoke safety with,
or insight into the next hour's possibilities.
they ran w/out food, soap, sanitary napkins, or
a change of underwear.

sometimes they ran with babies in their wombs, or the burnt
memory of babies that were auctioned right off their tits.
they out-ran death sometimes, didnt most times
& fell mercilessly back into the whip-filled reality of
bein owned by beings who walked on two legs
but were far lower than anything that ever crawled on four.
they ran with moses when they were lucky & with God
when they werent
carryin nothin but **the blood of ancestors** who refused to be
out-numbered or out-gunned into oblivion.

w/out reeboks, nikes or addidas
they ran thru wooded nightmares, swam thru misogynistic
rivers, plunged into hopeless swamps, & escaped into
a wilderness full of tricksters
who fed on their dreams & pigged-out on their humanity
til they became bigger parasites than the ones
who chased them outa dixie.

Being A Strong Black Woman

THEY SAY...

yr trinidadian friends say u used me.
that you were more interested in life in amerika,
than the life
in my eyes.
they say u lied about wanting me
that yr movements were more about backstroking
to amerika than deep stroking **into me.**
they say i was just a victim of yr silver tongue
a prisoner of yr carribean psyche
they say u were just after my money
but they dont know that for what u do to me
i wldve paid u double to do it **longer & stronger.**
they say u lied about loving me
but they were not there the night
we cursed each otha & instead of going home
u slept in my vestibule
while i curled up on the floor by the door
til the rhythm of yr breathing lured me
to sleep.
they werent there when your genitals
dropped their disguise to apologize
all lies were destroyed by the fire
that emanated from us
burning rubber inside each otha.
they werent there to see that yr con
was not half as long as the smoldering iron
u used to seal yrself into my honey jar.
only my tongue marks on yr swollen parts
cld be engaged to decipher the hieroglyphics
u inscribed on my vaginal walls
& it doesn't matter to me that they cldnt see

Can Get U Killed

how my nipples kept attacking yr mouth
forcing u to go south
til my back arched to the sky
& the only trace of a lie was me **screaming**
that i'd had enuff.

nobody knows what we weave
when i play loom to yr threading
nobody knows how u feel when u enter my black forest
& yr pulsating explorations
bring on the showers that cause my soul to shudder.

 all they kno is what they perceive to be
thousands & thousands of miles wedged between us
& they concoct those miles into a brew
that makes them drunk enough to swear
that u lied about wanting me
shammed about loving me
& though their words rub salt into
the wounds yr absence inflicts
not even amnesia can make me forget
the nights u maneuvered as if my thighs
were the red sea & u parted me
til the muscle of yr affections
plunged into my vulva-layers
taking the real truth
to my inner-most core.

Being A Strong Black Woman

MUST PEACE HAVE A GENDER?

indigo is the night
a star-studded painting by an artist
in luv with nocturnal splendor
which is
cool in its cleanliness/deep
in its own mystery.
the night is full of bodies that want to
bellydance under a virgin moon,
slow-drag under a sable sky
where the wetness of creation
hovers in the air
& only natural hair
can be decorated with celestial beads of joy
so why cant i groove
walk my sultry walk down city streets
letting the fingers of darkness stroke me
into a state of blessed peace?

becuz this is amerika
& no matter how much beauty flaunts itself after midnight
i'm a woman
& i'd better keep my butt in the house.

Can Get U Killed

THE DESCENT OF A FALLEN ANGEL
(for Robert Adams)

among the falling angels, u were the first to
tear the blinders from my eyes. i had no idea
that this AIDS thing was so deeeeep!
that yr so-called friends wld run away
that yr so-called mother wld hide
that yr so-called lover wld turn hetero.

i heard yr soul was on the run,
so i went looking for u, & found u in
johns hopkins, the hospital most Blks were
afraid to go to, cuz we all knew they wld use us
for experimentation whenever they got the chance.

i found u, skinnier than u had the right to be
i found u, losing yr eyesight & cursing yr insight
i found u, molding inside of yr smart mouth
i found u, blistering on the exterior, &
fermenting in the interior.
i found u
alone.

mary & thornton were the only columns left
of the temples u had erected. & i wedged
myself in between

not becuz we were allllll that close, but becuz
nobody shld die alone. & u needed to kno
that God, was not punishing u for being gay,
cuz the real Creator doesnt work that way.
u needed to know that the people who wont stay
dont count. & the ones that do

Being A Strong Black Woman

are the only flowers worth cultivating in yr
garden.

when i found u, u grabbed my hand &
begged me not to leave, like i was going somewhere.
& when i reached to hug u,
u pulled away, as if i cld catch what was having
the hell out of u.

& when i ignored yr caution, i felt yr soul let out
a sigh that came from someplace i hope
i'll never have to discover in myself.

u didnt know that AIDS had already eaten
my father alive. & that i was not afraid...
to hold u, massage u, or fold u delicately inside
my heart's safe-keeping.
i was not afraid, becuz whenever i do good,
i always feel like i've got coverage.

how yr life cld just leak out of a hole in yr being,
i will never understand. **u were the bomb!**
brains. looks. money. creativity. & thensome
but, there was always this sadness, this
ineffable thing that hovered over u.

u always lived on the fringes,
always tryed to balance yrself on the fence,
never fully black or white
never totally male or female, never just plain
happy or sad.

i luv'd u becuz u were the first person to make
me understand who i was, & that i was worthy

Can Get U Killed

of being luv'd.
u let me read my sorrowful pomes to u
& never suggested that i get a life.
u let me talk about my sorrowful lovers,
& never suggested that maybe i shld try
a woman.

u always took me just the way i came,
& that's why it was
so fitting for me to be with u in the end
not to keep the door from closing, but
to keep it from SLAMMING!

i didnt bother to go to yr funeral
cuz i knew it wld be filled with deserters
whining & crying as if they were auditioning
for a greek tragedy. & i had already said
my good-byes
slowly
articulately
& w/out drama.

Being A Strong Black Woman

CAN WE TALK?

can we talk

i have syllables that need to be performed
on the inside of yr thigh.
nouns that need the adjectives
of yr groans to push them into
exclamations of great joy.

can we talk

i know u wanna verb me & i wanna adverb u
right back, until all the question-marks
that we've ever harbored conjugate themselves
into an epicurean nectar
that only libertines can drink from.

can we talk

consonant on vowel, taut on soft, ear on mouth
can we hyphenate our own sobs & torture the complexity
of our grammatical gasps & screams
shrieking with pure delight.

can we talk

about the crossroads—those points where
our doings meet to commemorate our sexual oppositeness
when embellished to the highest possible demonstrative degree.

can we talk

cuz i dont have any flights scheduled for tonite
& we both know how badly u wanna get into the sky.

Can Get U Killed

THE TRANE THEY CLDNT DE-RAIL

bustin out of n. carolina like a runaway train
john redefined the saxophone—made it do things
that were IMpossible... blew the notes
out in somersaults, upside down, inside out,
while landin in perfect harmony.

his personal life was once so fraught with oppression
that only poppies & smoky melodies
cld untwist the coils of passion
that trapped his creativity &
threatened
to take the T of his tenor.

trane was a malcolm with a horn
strikin chords of agonizin sounds like slaves
beatin on freedom's door.
he turned our anger & frustration into musical sagas
that pale hipsters wanted to tap w/out experiencin.
when the riots reached historical proportions
his music fingerpainted the background
where we dueled with the devil over control
of our own hearts & minds.

when 4 angels from alabama were recalled
to heaven, w/out our permission, he turned
himself into tears that we cld all shed
w/out bein devastated.

trane captured my favorite things & turned them
over to us for our revolutionary utilization.
he rescued the ballads & returned them to the
earth's original HeArT-ThRoBbErS.

Being A Strong Black Woman

he coupled with johnny hartman & together
they assassinated the myth of the blk man bein
incapable of expressin luv while makin
sinatra look over his shoulder & give thanx
that he was wite & in charge.

trane was a healer, a high-priest who led us into
the temples of our own mortality, where the act of
breathin was a holy happenin constantly endangered
by jealous fiends born w/out ears.

even durin his most troubled days,
he was more than an instrument of good, he was
a conduit of the raw energy reflected in the eyes of the
exploited masses, so eager to return to greatness.

even when the villains of melody tried continuously
to stifle his nile-like flow, he was a journey agent of escape
for 20th century urban cotton-pickers,
still bein checked by polyester-suited overseers
with cellular whips.

with liberated tunes, he cleared spaces in our hearts
& filled them with the peace—that sanity, needed to exist
he touched our spirits with godliness, when even
God seemed to be on sabbatical.

trane was the vehicle, layin down new tracks on the
underground railroad, & we rode his atomic harmonies
into outer-space where there was no oppression
no melanin deficient bandits tryin to strip the poly
from our rhythms & no afrikan hatin deities
crucifyin the purity of our sun-songs.

Can Get U Killed

trane's ultra-divine riffs executed the demons of racism
castrated the whoremongerin Blue Notes
& cocooned us into the vibratory frequency of

a Love Supreme.

ONLY ENUFF IS ENUFF

to **singe** the skin is not **enuff**
i want
my eyes to go back up in my head
til the red alert
of my being goes all the way off!

makin my heart beat
in places hotter than my chest
is not gonna do it tonite.
i wanna impress the devil
& make **fire** fall on its knees
to me.

 sketches in pyrotechnics
will only make me pump up the volume
& if yr tongue hasnt danced by midnight
everything u had hoped to ride
will vanish
& what u wake up holdin
will truly be yr own.

Can Get U Killed

FORGIVENESS WILL COME, BUT NOT TODAY
(For Arsell Robinson)

in the goring 20's
people cld hardly walk down the streets of chicago
w/out wonderin if a sicilian-coated bullet
wld interrupt their journey
& drop-kick them into a premature grave.

fast-forwardin into baltimore, 70 years later
my cousin is comin out of a store
& is ambushed by a bullet that caps an end
to his entire assortment of dreams.

to u with the ignorant trigger finger
to u/to whom maat is obviously unknown
what were u usin for thought
the day u robbed a store, jumped
into a car
& just shot aimlessly out of the window
during the getaway.

u just shot out of the window
didnt even note whether it was a man
woman or a child, spasmin against the might
of yr projectile.
u didnt even look to see SURPRISE rip
his body apart, while u & yr make-shift manhood
yee-haa'd toward a karma
that wld tax a lovin God's imagination.

u fool
u rancid mutation of a turd
u deaf, dumb & blind reject from a slime factory

Being A Strong Black Woman

u 20th century, super-bubonic plague infested cretin
u fugitive from sanity & grace
u poor example of pharonic greatness
shittin on itself.

u just shot out of the fuckin window!.
didnt aim. didnt stare down the sights at someone
u hated to the nth degree
u just shot out of the window
didnt even give him the courtesy of a contemptuous look.
u cldnt even curse his name as u pulled the trigger
cuz u didnt kno it.
u just shot out of the window
& put a hole in my family, the size of the grand canyon.

if u hated life so much
why didnt u just pop a cap in yr own butt
& excuse yr way outa here.

the all-consumin awareness
of my ancestors has cursed me
with a luv so unconditionally afrikan
that some of it even has to spill over onto u.

i cant wish u pain/cuz
obviously, that's all u've ever known
i cant wish u were dead
cuz u've never lived.

i wish God wld pry open yr eyes with revelations
so u can salvage some part of yr own worth OR
i wish u an earlier expiration date &
the deliberate absence of the ancestors
at yr arrival into the halls of eternity.

Can Get U Killed

THE WARRIOR

what the warrior is
she is. no matter how much
u try to pink her, betty-boo her,
declitorize, or pastel her.
her ability to fight to the finish
cannot be mascectomied or hysterwrecktomied away
her ability to define herself, even in the face of death
cannot be
neutralized by super-sonic acrobatics in & out
of her vagina.

 what the warrior is
she is. no matter how many times
her womb yields, her shields & spears are always in place.
there is nothin she wont do to defend the human-race
& she will always resemble yr mother.

Being A Strong Black Woman

SORRY, I DIDNT CATCH WHAT
U WERE SAYIN, I WAS TOO BUSY
LISTENIN TO MY DICK

"what was it u were sayin, baby?"
"it hurts?"
"u dont feel like it?"
"u might have a little yeast?"
"did i pull the tip on the rubber?"
"u stopped takin the pill?"
"u didnt cum?"
"oh."

ALL'S FAIR ....

i'm not tryin to be a feminist, or anything like that
but, can i command yr nipples the way u do mine
i mean fair is fair.
so, wld u mind removin yr shirt
so i can impose my will upon those tight little tits
that strain to feel my tongue
so they can stiffen with apprehension at the thought
of what i might do next.

i'm sure u kno it aint just a woman's thing
so dont get upset when u feel my teeth dancin
around those dark, tasty seedlings that threaten to JUMP
off yr chest
when pressed just right between the shameless lips
of an intoxicatin mouth.

i promise not to tell how high u jump
if u'll just let me sky-rocket yr nipples
with a thousand thirsty kisses that leave u suckin on air
while i throw back my hair & prepare
to take no prisoners!

Being A Strong Black Woman

MICHAEL

developed expressly for display
given the race memory of a clone
cultivated for pop-human consumption
wants to be left alone
to ramble in the one-dimensional garden
he rents in the twilight zone
where, it is rumored, he bargains
in the millions to possess the elephant man's bones,
a being for whom he has a natural affinity.

starting with the man in the mirror
he attacked every hint of his own genetic make-up
as **payback** to the people
who obviously hurt him most.

& as he moon-walks toward slicker millions
& more madness, we wonder
if he'll ever forgive us
for letting them castrate him
w/out a fight.

THE PERIOD

yes, i have a period.
& it goes where i go.
i do not whisper about it, or call it cute
little names to disguise it.

i have a period.
at times, i might even bleed thru my clothes
w/out excusin myself.
i have no problems askin for tampons, in a store, full of men.

i have a period.
& we've been togetha now for at least 30 yrs.
i dont bother wishin it wld just go away,
cuz the fact that it comes is usually a clear signal
that i am not inhabited.

i have a period.
& if u wanna be with me, u'll just have to accept that
i might ask u to go get tampons for me.
i might ask u to rub my stomach if i have cramps.
i might tell u no, becuz luvin may be too messy

i have a period.
& it does not make me unclean, or too impure
to cook or simply touch anotha human bein.
it does not make me weaker, or dumber, or less than myself.
becuz when i'm on, i am standin in the center of my power.
& anybody, who has a problem with that, can roll out
& put a period behind that!

Being A Strong Black Woman

CAUGHT BY A DIABOLICAL RUBY

with integrated toes, the wholistic prostitutes
tipped hauntingly thru the mists of the athiestic ocean
anxious to act out fairy-tales written by illiterate pimps.
in the mouth-watering shadows of scrumptious pyramids
they danced like presumptuous swans
caught in the enchanting glass clarity of a
diabolical ruby that made promises of silk & soul
    but in the end was
    brutally **leather.**

FOR NTOZAKE:
QUEEN OF THE COLORED GIRLS

a lot of people kno what u do
& they dont like it.

they like to read u as if yr pomes were just words
they dont want to kno how much u paid for them.
they dont want to kno why u do what u do
they just wanna reap the benefits.
they are very passionate in thinkin
u abuse substances, but care nothin
about the substances that abuse u.
they wanna pay u some bullshit honorarium
& later, sit back & listen while u punk-slap them
into the realities they tunnel vision out of daily.

a lotta people get excited when they hear yr name
& shut-down completely at the price u pay
to satisfy their literary libidos.
they think u shld *just say no*
yet remain open to the constant rape of yr
carefully whetted, 24-carat sensibilities.

some people think yr pomes are just some shit
u make up when u feelin sorry for yrself
they dont care to kno that u are an astute chronicler
of human sufferin, trapped between
beauty's extremities.
what do they kno, readin safely
with eyes that function perfectly in rooms that
do not reflect?
they wanna question yr habits

Being A Strong Black Woman

declare u a good writer, *but*
an artistic genius, **but**
a nobel prize-winning possibility,*but*
a masterful wordologist, *but*...

they dont kno or care how the pomes pick u
how they ride u til u yield & yr guts
are splattered all over the page & ignorantly
written off as prose— the blood notwithstandin.

they think u make all that shit up
cuz they too one-dimensional to kno that
u are the missin children's screams unmuffled
the beat-up sistah's unchained melody
the tortured revolutionary's inaudible cries.

they think u make allll that shit up
cuz they too numb to kno
—everything u write about
u live about.
& no pome wearin truth comes forth w/out exactin
from u an incredible price that no amount of royalties
or awards can ever balance out.

a lotta people claim they luv yr work
but they dont like what they **think** u do
but i say, when luv is real, it encompasses all
& i take u anyway u come, so much so,
if the absolute radiance of u cld be contained
in a single gem, i wld place u on my altar
& dare anyone to speak yr name
unless **praying.**

Can Get U Killed

SHE GOTTA REAL BIG MOUTH

in terms of where i've been
& the shit i've had to take
from beings who consider breasts
a sure indicator of inferiority,
what i have absorbed
makes my blood clot.

the misery i have withstood
hardens within like a fibroid tumor
that dares surgery & pollutes
my blood with sexist notions that make
the beastina in me read a fool into filth
at the drop of a tampon.

Being A Strong Black Woman

I AM THE BLOOD QUEEN

i am the captive of an evil tumor-king
who wants to devour me & lease my blood out
to his red-crossed friends.

i am the blood queen
i am the chosen one, swimming in my own juices
while the kingdom celebrates my inability to just jump
on my horse & ride into menopause.

i am the blood queen
spirals of red ooze down my legs
balanced unhappily between
the crystals oozing down my cheeks
i am emersed in red fantasies of dancing divas
without wombs, castrated poets
without voices.

i am the blood queen
amazing the world with my super-simba menstrual powers
& the relentless way i flow
without calling for help—while worlds of tampons
crumble and die right in my face
which is also between my thighs.

i am the blood queen
my flows are legendary
and my sheets never lie.

Can Get U Killed

NOW THAT RECIPROCITY IS A HOTEL
ON FANTASY ISLAND

having offered u all
endless luv
endlessly
& getting in return
the concern
that comes only
when notification must be sent
about a family emergency,

i shed the skin
that needed to identify with u so much!
i willingly yield to the reality
that yr luv for me
has a gaping hole in it
i walk away ... from u all
with no guilt.

Being A Strong Black Woman

KARMA

all i wanna kno is, did i hurt people?
did i take their luv & smash it against the windows
of their souls? did i violate someone?
did i rape revolutionaries?
did i steal from churches & temples?
WHAT!
cld i have done to deserve meeting u?

was i a wrongful war veteran? did i sell drugs?
did i squeal on nat turner?
was i an overseer? did i make babies with my own children?
WHAT?
cld i ever have done, to deserve meeting u?

did i pimp children? did i willingly sleep with massah tom?
did i help frame garvey?
did i sell blk people to wite people for their pleasure?
did i help guide the goddamn ships in?
WHAT!
cld i possibly have done to deserve meeting u?

Can Get U Killed

I DONT GET BLU, I GET THE HORRORS

they came like a shower of boils
jumped on me like a thousand crazi bitches
dragged my inflamed memory around by the hair
& shoved my well-honed reasoning out of a
third floor window.

armed in white cloth, shields of ammonia,
& daggers of salt—i sent the boils back to the sender
drove the bitches back into hell
rescued my abused memory & patched
my reasoning back together with rosewater & faith.

standing in the crack between the worlds
i declare to spirits known & unknown
that there's nothing u can do to me that
cant be undone. & as long as my ancestors
have my back, i not only ENdure,
but PREvail & OVERwelm!

Being A Strong Black Woman

IS YR GOD WORTH DEFENDIN?

when somebody bombs yr church
that's just their way of sayin,
FUCK U
&
FUCK YR GOD, too.

its July, 1996
& again, the spotlight is on us
& again, the molotoff cocktails are bein
mixed for us.
& again, we go cryin to the u.s. govt
the same govt that amassed great wealth
at our endurin expense & then
put us to the curb.
the same govt that creates the magnificent mazes
that we are welcome to scurry thru
everyday of our rat-like lives,
til we either find our way out
or die along the path.

again, we are the targets for dumb-ass cracker bullshit
theories that they, the real wretched of the earth,
had to construct to explain why they are so pitifully situated
at the core of amerika's anus.

again, **we stood up,** marched
a million men thru d.c.
& the payment for our marchin is bein
exacted in the form of desecrated holy places.
places that house our souls while providin a haven

Can Get U Killed

for our run-away minds —which are constantly bein
chased by the blood-hounds of dingy wite supremacy.

we can march a million thru d.c., but
we cant march a million to alabama-georgia?
we can rally around abstractions, but

we cant rally against the concreteness
of somebody **spittin on our God?**
our young men draw guns on each otha everyday
but we cant stop the enemy from bombin our churches?
our youth are watchin us with **eagle-eyes**, waitin
to see what we're gonna do, & all we've done
is wear out our knees.

& i'm not tryin to mock prayer
but prayer w/out action is a mockery in itself.
why shld God be willin to do more for us
than we are willin to do for ourselves.

we're under attack again, & what do we do
we stand in the pulpit, cryin & wringin our hands out
to a God who must surely be tired of our whinin by now.
we drag our faces around, beggin for compassion
pleadin for an end to that which will never end
until we end it!

i dont want to belong to a church
that tells me i have to be good to people who treat me
like shit!
idont want a minister whose sermons dont inspire me
to protect & defend my own. i dont want a minister
who tells me that i have two cheeks.
iwant a minister like nat turner.

Being A Strong Black Woman

i want a minister who insures me that God has my back
whenever i go to war in her/his name.
if prayer was the key to liberation
we wld've been double-free 400 yrs ago.
dont nobody pray more than blk folks...
we probably gotta direct line to the Most High,
when what we need is a direct line to each otha.

i dont agree with Farrakahn's everythin
but u can bet, if he called for a forum concernin the bombings
even our enemies wld think anotha thought
before they mixed up anotha demolition brew.

& where's the right reverend such & such
hystorically, his mouth has been in everythin but a hearse
& now when the battle has finally reached his arena
where is he? over in the middle east tryin to free
some hostages? is he vacationin in "hymie-town"?
where is the minister of ministers?
the grand puba of opportunism?
the matinee-idol of blk theology?
guaranteed to show up wherever there's a show-down
but mute & invisible to the people who need him now.

& where's reverend so & so?
the fire & brimstone has arrived prematurely, bro
where's yr bible?
hope u didnt leave it at the naacp headquarters.
hope u didnt leave it on her bedroom floor.
hope u can leave the women alone long enuff
to grab yr asbestos suit & head down south
i kno u aint gonna let anybody thrash the pulpits
of our collective divinity

Can Get U Killed

w/out at least goin to verbal war.
right bro? am i right?

now that we're on the subject, where
are the members of the ministers' club?
i hope y'all aint in d.c. grovelin
at the holocaust museum
the one our tax dollars helped to build
the one that only acknowledges the jewish experience
the one that refuses to recognize the native amerikans'
hellacaust—the one that denies the afrikan maafa!
i kno y'all aint at the museum—pleadin with the jews
to help u/cuz if it werent for the slave ships they financed
many of us wldnt be here now.
so if they pledge their help—better turn it upside down
& inside out, cuz they never help anybody
w/out receivin the greater benefit.

but excuse me if i've digressed
cuz the real issue here is
aint our God worth defendin?

how can any of us show up in church
next sunday, or any sunday—knowin
that our places of worship are under fire
& all our pitiful rhetoric does
is fan the flames.
shall we call in the national guard
or the fruit of islam?
do we wait for the calvary
or do we clean our rifles?
do we fight fire with fire—or do we
hide under the pews & wait for slick willie
to legislate us into safety?

Being A Strong Black Woman

the time for waitin for someone to come to our rescue
is gone—matter of fact, it never was
we dont need anybody's permission to defend ourselves
we dont need anybody else's money to pay for our defense.
& if we truly luv God the way our songs & sermons say we do
then we need to throw off our vintaged fears
straighten our backs, check our ammo,
& get ready to either rock & roll with the devil
or meet our Maker with a high-five.

ASSASSIN

i was born to be an assassin
stealthy.
critical.
a killer of any imagery that
gnaws at the souls of my people.

i was born to be deadly
to disengage, deactivate, & destroy
any missiles containing seeds of self-hatred
that might be aimed
at the souls of my people.

i was born to murder
wreak havoc
annihilate
any person, place, or thang
that makes my people
question the beauty in themselves.

i was born an assassin
easy to detonate
impossible to dismantle
my movements toward justice are so swift
they escape my own observation.

IDA

wite people have never been sexist
about destroyin blk people
they'll kill a woman
just as quick
as they'll kill a man.

& becuz she understood this
& did not leave herself accessible
to freedom's 19th century hype
Ida
padded her hips with six-shooters
& demanded that the devil
find some otha place for a luncheon
besides a blkman's lynchin.

& when the demons came ridin in
hidin behind soiled sheets
she hid behind the ancestors
& wld disappear from wite-sight
into the safety of a blk panther nite.

Can Get U Killed

OUT

whatdya mean out?

aint no out in here. only IN
if you knew u wanted to be out, u shlda never
came in here, cuz here likes you, very much
& she aint inclined to release that which
fills her & scorches her
by denying herself a precisioned stroke...

OUT is for people who really didn't care
cldnt really hang,
IN is for the silky-muscled lance
that u plunge with so intensely, making the spirit of muscles
past contract & grasp the significance of why
orgasms not war, shld be the national past-time.

OUT?

where did u get that from?
was it something u read/something u saw in the movies
OUT is for people who live in the twilight zone
people who think sex is in & out & round about
dip & dab & dont come back.

my IN
has been waiting for you since yr first wet-dream
& right now, we still have seams to bust & fireworks to create
suns to outshine & earthquakes to maintain
if u pull out now, it'll never be the same.

Being A Strong Black Woman

OUT

i hope that's a new position? if so, spare me, cuz
i'm still caught up in the rarity of u wanting me as severely
as i want u.

OUT, there's no getting out of here
didnt u see the bodies strewn around the bed
or werent u paying attention?

OUT is an abstraction
an aberration
cruel & unusual punishment
suitable only for a child of a lesser god.

IN is where yr strength belongs
churning in the perfect
center of a vulva orchid
designed with yr mojo in mind
custom-made to flawlessly fit
every gyration in yr imagination.

understand

when it comes to the ins & outs of
outrageous fleshing
there is only IN
deepER
& deepEST
& by the time u hit that last stroke
u'll be wearing my IN like u wear yr own skin.

& as our nerve-endings wrestle across
the satiny portals of the great climax zone .

Can Get U Killed

our flame-licked bodies
ease up on the contortions
& we stare breathlessly at each otha
knowing

that if OUT comes, u will refuse.

IN SEARCH OF. . . .

Serious Black Woman
ISO
sensitive Native Amerikan
to apologize to
for the blood we drew
when we were brain-damaged.

Serious Black Woman
ISO
forgiving Native Amerikan
to bridge cultures with
while restoring the legacy
of the mixed blood
within.

Serious Black Woman
ISO
informed Native Amerikan
who is not afraid to track
the footsteps of our ancestors
back into the everglades of
those lost worlds
where once
we luv'd each otha.

Can Get U Killed

OUR LADY OF THE SLAMMER

night after night after night
for u alone, i am ambience
wistfully voluptuous
somber & wild.
nocturnal restlessness
finds me comin from under yr cot
where i exist not
until yr secrets summon me
yr oiled hand invokes me
yr hunger for freedom shapes me
while yr un-luv'd self violently
impales me upon the crying edge
of yr penis
& luvin u only, i die...
night after night after night
until yr cell-mate out appeals u &
takes me with greater desperation
into the hastily greased grasp of his
more brutalized soul
& night after night after night
the prayers of caged dark men
are what i live to answer.

Being A Strong Black Woman

ALMOST EROTIKA BLUES

if it's one thang i cant stand,
its a beggar. a whiner.
a please, baby, baby, can i-man, who cant
longer than 15 mtes, w/out
fallin off dead to sleep.

if there's one thang i cant abide
its a semi-hard lover
who just keeps pumpin away as if
my coochie is too stupid to kno
that the party's over, or at least postponed.

if there's one thang that ticks me off
it's seein someone's face move lovingly
down my torso & beyond my navel
& into where he winds up lappin up
on everythang but the right thang.

& nothin can be worse than
feelin myself nearin the heat of ecstasy
only to be shot down by a
"damn, baby. that sure was good!"
& the look on my hand when it realizes
it'll have to finish the job, alone.

Can Get U Killed

EVEN THE RIGHTEOUS
MUST APOLOGIZE SOMETIMES
(For Leonard Peltier)

when we, as afrikan people, call the world into account
for all the heinous transgressions loosed upon us,
we are poignantly articulate
eloquently exact
and agonizingly repetitious, yet
when it comes to reckoning with what
we've done to othas, we are
pathetically, quiet.

every time we volunteered on a campaign
every time we chased, harassed or trapped the native amerikan
we were wrong!

dont sing no songs bout buffalo soldiers to me
unless u're gonna tell the whole truth.
we shlda been fighting on the buffalo's side
trying to exterminate the people who were exterminating them.

every time we let the wite man tell us who to kill
every time we out-zealed him in his lust for the hunt of the
native amerikans
we were dead wrong!

& that fact will be with us & be with us ... until
we confront the remaining tribes & ask
from the nucleus of our afrikanity for forgiveness
the kind that we can see & celebrate at least once a year
on their territory or ours
whichever one we liberate first.

Being A Strong Black Woman

IT'S OKAY SAYS THE FDA

back again, after a brief hiatus in the 3rd world
the makers of the pill, the iud, & the
tuskegee experiment
bring u **norplant.**

guaranteed, to enhance the quality of yr life
by eliminating the possibility of un-wanted
pregnancies for 5 years.
& if u dont go blind, grow hair on yr chin,
discharge from yr breast, bleed incessantly,
or start eating like a pig
then u will kno that
norplant is the one for u.

dont let yr friends be the only ones to have fun
u too can experience the independence
& false sense of assuredness that can come with the use of
nature's little helper, the blessed norplant.
guaranteed to make u a social butterfly
as long as u dont lose handfuls of yr hair
cough up blood, faint, or become severely depressed
u too can be popular with **norplant.**

 be the first one in yr crowd
to plant 5 years worth of drugs in yr system
& if yr arm doesnt drop off & yr womb
doesnt fall out
u will be the envy of allll yr friends.

this commercial was paid for & sponsored by
the same people who brought yr ancestors to these shores.

Can Get U Killed

TRUTH IS THE ONLY EXORCIST

the spirit of a dead buffalo soldier
has somehow possessed the soul of my brotha
the part-time yo. at times, he just zaps out!
starts talkin in tongues about what he'd do
if his cuntry went to war.
his eyes get all big & glassy
& u can tell there's somethin evil makin him say those things
cuz he aint even got a cuntry
& the only safe place he ever knew was in his momma's womb.

sometimes, that spirit be workin him
& he starts talkin bout how he help'd put the **wipeout**
on the native amerikans, & he figures on doin the same thing
to the cubans if Fidel gets anymore out of hand.
he's so strung out on red, white, & blue
that he dont even realize, that most of the folks
amerika attacks, look just like him.

the spirit of a gung-ho buffalo soldier
is movin towards murder, while wearin my brotha's face.
& day after day, I read black history aloud
tryin to invoke truth strong enuff to cast the buffalo soldier
from the bodies of all my bros.
to make them impervious to the lies amerika tells them, on
every newscast, on every tabloid.
daily dosages of afriknology are the only majik i kno
to absolve the murders we've committed in all the wars
amerika has suckered us into fightin ... only knowledge
of afrikan history can make the spirit of the buffalo soldier
remain in the past where deeds done in ignorance
can be stamped: DO NOT REPEAT

Being A Strong Black Woman

WERE U THERE WHEN THEY CRUCIFIED MY LORD

if we rounded up all the men in the Nation
and scrutinized them to the nth degree
we still wldnt find one malcolm.
if we took all the speeches spoken by all the blk leaders since
1965, they cld not illuminate our reality more than the words left
by malcolm.
if we combined all
the post-garvey fears of wite people and laid them down
at the feet of the one
whose truths terrorized them the most,
it wld have to be malcolm.

for malcolm was our lord of liberation.
he was the alpha & omega of blk manhood. the answer
to the mystery of the sphinx. the uncontested paradigm
of metamorphosis. the first pharoah to unite upper and lower self.
the buddha of ebony consciousness.
the christ of analytical persuasion.

did he walk on water, no, he walked on fire.
did he feed the masses with seven loaves & seven fish, no,
he fed hungry minds with facts & figures.
did he make the lame walk, no,
he made the challenged realize their power.
did he suffer the little children to come unto him, no,
he took healing to the streets and embraced all ages.
did he challenge the scribes & the pharisees, no,
he debated with all of racist amerika, & trapped them in the nets
of their own lies.
did he raise lazarus from the dead, no,
he raised a million lazarus's from a million ghetto graves.
did he teach people to love their enemies,no,

Can Get U Killed

he showed his people
how to luv themselves.
did he rise from death after the third day, no,
he stripped death of its power & stepped into the gloryfield
of his peerless ancestors.

were u there when they crucified my lord?

were u in the house when uncle tomism came full circle
to surround our prince of peace.
were u on yr way to the ballroom when the low-lifed,
punk-ass pistoleros took their seats. where was security when
our lord entered his final hours.
where were the police
when time & circumstance descended upon
our annointed one. where was elijah when his real son
was being lined up on the cross.

were u there when they crucified my lord?

were u behind the stage when destiny lured him out
into the open.
were u stitting near his children
when fatherlessness claimed them.
did u smell the fear in his stomach as he pressed forward
into infinity.
were his eyes glassy.
were his movements jerky.
when he as-salaam-alaikum'd,did he stutter.
when somebody screamed, get yr hand outa my pocket,
did u jump.
when the steel thunder of shotguns filled the audubon ballroom,
did u hit the floor.
did u run towards him or away.

Being A Strong Black Woman

when his blood burst forth from the various holes,
did u go into shock, did u throw up, or were u too paralyzed
to move. when his body
went limp & slid to the floor,
where were the cpr trainees. where was the f.o.i.
where was the o.a.a.u., where was farrakhan, where was shorty,
where were the warriors! where was n.y.'s finest, where were the
fbi infiltraters, where was elijah, where was justice,
where was allah.

were u there when they crucified our lord?

when all the poems have been perpetrated. when all the dirges
have been sung.
the memory of our steel-boned warlord,will come to us in our
darkest hour & make us try ourselves for his murder.
for we are guilty of having been too human to save him.
we are guilty of letting his killers live.
we are guilty of paying tribute to those who executed him
not by pulling the trigger, but by giving the final order
& creating the atmosphere to make it so.
we are guilty of allowing amerika to
downplay his legacy.
we are guilty of not supporting his wife & children.
we are guilty of not honoring his sistah ella.
we are guilty of
allowing farrakhan to profane mosque #7 by
letting one of malcolm's convicted murderers take over
the very temple he built into prominence.
we are guilty of
letting amerika badmouth him
& then put his face on a postage stamp.
we are guilty of not making his birthday

Can Get U Killed

a universal holiday.
we are all guilty of not loving him half as much as he
passionately luv'd us.

& if anybody out there thinks that malcolm was not one of the
greatest, most fearless, warrior-scholars of this century
my friend, u've been misled, bambuzzled, hoodwinked.

STILL THE FIRE

age emulates seasons
a proper way of being marks every passage.
a junior elder, now savoring the last of summer
i approach words differently,
use less, mean more
which is not to say that my pomes are losing their fire
but, where once they kindled
now they stoke.

WHERE GOD LIVES

tobago, in the mountains, in the morning
is a misty entrapment of mango-scented peace
the absence of stress seeps into the pores
& drives the soul into breathless ascension.

tobago, in the mountains, in the morning
inspires a total awareness of being
internal fireworks go off, causing a sudden
surge of connectedness/a cataclymic loss of I-ness.

tobago, in the mountains, in the morning
flushes & rejuvenates/purges & invigorates
urging the higher self to emerge in gratitude
at being able to embrace the place
where GOD lives.

Being A Strong Black Woman

BEFORE U GO IN SEARCH OF

if u'd like to melt in luving arms that yearn
to be wrapped around u, then use the ones closest,
& hug yrself. if u'd like to be thrilled by a tender kiss,
try touching the salty/sweetness of yr own skin,
with yr own eager mouth. if u'd like to have a gentle foot rub,
then take the hands u receive so well with,
& massage yr own feet til every sinew sighs with relief.

if u'd like to slip into an element of irresistible peace, then
take a candle-lit bath, spiced with healing herbs
& self-appreciation.
if u'd like to receive a bouquet of exotic flowers &
the message of caring they bring, then buy some
& remember that flowers kno no gender.

if u'd like to be wined & dined, then treat yrself to
an evening out & be grateful for the company.
if u want a lover that will never forsake u for anotha,
then luv yrself & have a partner for life.

Can Get U Killed

TIL YR ASHES GIVE THANKS

luv is usually an unexpected phenomena
it conceives itself, wherever, whenever, however it wants
any two pair of eyes can collide on a prepaid ride to a place
their combined imaginations cld not have evoked in a million
octavia butler years.

luv is completely irrational
it controls its own barometer
& never feels compelled to explain itself to anyone.

luv is strictly autonomous, dwelling securely
within itself, marking time in its own fashion.
working reality according to its own needs.

luv is self-reliant
there are no circumstances upon which it depends
luv has nothing up its sleeve
but is always guaranteed to pull a rabbit up outa its hat.
luv is a creature of infinate disguises
multiple personalities & baptist choir drama.
luv is yr self looking right back at u
when u're in no mood for introspection.

luv is culturally deprived
thinks nothing of protocol & doesnt give a damn
about what otha people think.

luv never thinks straight becuz it has nothing to think with
its more two-faced than a childhood friend
will tell yr mind one thing, & tell yr heart anotha.

Being A Strong Black Woman

luv is the original gangster
will pop a sugar-coated cap up in u &
have u hip-hopping & be-bopping at the same time.
no matter how bad u think u are, it'll stick u up
take everything u have, & leave u talkin jibberish
while u wait in limbo for a heart-transplant.

luv is what the whole world needs, & doesnt kno what to do with
on a good day, its everying u thought it wld be
on a bad day, its everything people tried to tell u.

luv is that kiss u kno u shldnt hang onto, but yr idiot lips
wont let go of. its a house on fire & instead of running out, u
run farther in, looking for the living-room
& a comfortable place to burn
til yr ashes, give thanks

UNTITLED

if u cant imagine a slave thinking slavery was good
or that one massah
was better then anotha
...imagine blk people favoring the democrats
over the republicans.

WHEN A SLAVE'S PRAYER WAS GREATER
THAN THE MASTERS' REALITY

when we were praying
for freedom
we were asking for something
even wite folks
didnt have
or understand.

LINEAGE

suppose we discovered that
donald duck
was really the son of mickey & minnie mouse,
we'd have a whole new slant on disneyland then,
wldnt we?

DIFFERENT STROKES

when a blk person marries a wite person
(even though its really vice-a-versa)
i usta act like i'd lost something.
what Spirit gives, cannot be taken away,
and no one can keep me from my blessings (liberation).
it took me a lot of teeth-grinding, eye-rolling &
fire-breathing pomes to realize, that when a blk person
marries a wite person,
nothing is taken away from me.
no lack is created in me becuz i have everything
i will ever need, always have & always will
& the responsibility of remembering that, is on me.
a blk person who wld marry a wite person
is obviously someone who has not experienced the world
the way i have.
is obviously not a member of my reality group.
so in their movement towards witeness
they take nothing from me, cuz
they werent giving me anything in the first place.

Can Get U Killed

BE SURE U'RE SURE

u're walkin down the street, in the land of the free
& the home of the brave
u see a blk man comin towards u
before yr fear forces u to cross the street
are u sure he's not a messiah?

u're walkin down the street
u see a wite man comin towards u
before u react to the weight of 400 years of terror
are u sure he's not an abolitionist?

u're walkin down the street
u see a spanish-speakin man comin towards u
before u move to protect yr territory
are u sure he's not bearin gifts?

u're walkin down the street
u see an asian comin towards u
before u flash back to pearl harbor or vietnam
are u sure he's not a buddha?

u're walkin down the street
u see a native-amerikan comin towards u
before u angrily go into denial over whose land this is
are u sure he's not a shaman?

u're walkin down the street
u see someone foreign comin towards u
before u stereo-type, stamp & reject
are u sure, he's not yr brotha?

Being A Strong Black Woman

PLAGUE

worms in the wheat
rats in the pantry
roaches in yr bed
germans in the carribean
how many more analogies do u need?

AND SO WE EAT

seeing ourselves as animals is too hard
so we forget on purpose, that animals
only eat when they're hungry
only eat when they need nourishment.

when our lives lack order, WE EAT. when we cant
put together a plan, WE EAT. when someone dies, WE EAT
when we hate our jobs, WE EAT. when we have no friends,
WE EAT. when we dont like the ones we have, WE EAT.
when we feel un-appreciated, WE EAT. when we feel
overwhelmed
WE EAT. when we dont want to attract sexual attention, WE
EAT
when we cant attract it, WE EAT.

when we cant read, WE EAT. when we can't afford to go out,
WE EAT. when we are unemployable, WE EAT.
when we watch the stories,
WE EAT. when we get high, WE EAT. when we stop getting
high, WE EAT.

when lovers fade into myths, WE EAT the space they ustah
occupy. when dreams start to crumble or flake,
we mix them with tears & eat them, w/out sugar.
when we cant control our children, WE EAT.
when we cant shake the memories from abusive childhoods,
WE EAT.when child-support doesnt come, WE EAT.
when we cant think clearly, WE EAT.
when we cant sleep, WE EAT.
WE EAT til we cant walk,

Being A Strong Black Woman

and when we cant walk, WE EAT.
WE EAT when we stop smoking cigarettes.

WE EAT when we cant lose weight.
everyday, some of us eat the dry crust of deferred dreams
& wash it down with the juice of self-loathing.

 no matter what we're really hungry for, WE EAT
& when WE EAT, we usually eat wrong.

HAIKU'S

1.

reap a field of bones
u one day will
pay for all
the lynchings u sowed.

2.

looking for more than
spanish will pay
yr soul learns
to beg in english.

3.

designer shoes on
restricted feet
nike chains
better than shackles.

Being A Strong Black Woman

A BLESSINGS-COUNTER

we all need a blessings-counter
someone, or thing that reminds us at various times of the day
of the blessings we need to be thankful for.

someone, or thing that will list in perfect detail all the things
we've got going for us.
someone, or thing that can help reveal
the lessons hiding in what appear to be the non-blessings
that we take for granted and/or ignore.

we all need a blessings-counter
so we can be on time giving praise before praise is overdue.
& since otha people always seem to kno more about our
blessings than we do
why dont we all be counters for one anotha
that way we'll be obliged to shout thanks every minute
sing hallelujahs
every hour.

Can Get U Killed

THE ICEMAN'S CONFESSION
(Inspired by John H. Clarke)

when i was born, u feared me
shrank away in terror & disgust/cldnt believe
i cld come from u.
when i was born, u with-held yr luv, based on the fact that
i didnt look the way u thought i shld.

soon after me, came othas, born to be undesirable, to be forever
outside. one day, we just up & took our rejected selves north
so north, we ended up in an ice land.
a place devoid of nurturing energy, a place unconducive to
human-life
a place that hated to share, a place too frigid to deny, too
horrible to acknowledge.
& there we stayed. surviving, the only way we knew how
eating anything that moved & didnt smell human.
& change ravished us!
unyielding frost down-sized our noses, glacial winds reduced
our lips to bare necessity.
the absence of sun brutalized our hair, & froze the melanin
right outa our eyes.
& there we evolved, knowing only lack
& disconnectedness.
worshipping fire, until all otha elements became superfluous
we lived, not becuz we luv'd life, but to spite the harsh climate
that kept telling us
to die.

& when the god of ice had calcified our pineal gland
& starved us down
to something, only vaguely human,

Being A Strong Black Woman

in search of food, we dragged ourselves out of the caves,
thru centuries of barbarism
& straight into afrika.
and BEHOLD, what did we find...a sable race of people
bidding us welcome. we, who had never been welcomed
anywhere/not even in each othas' eyes.
we, who knew only to take what we wanted before it disappeared.
we, who have never known abundance or reciprocity
were being welcomed into afrika, the mother of all humanity
the same mother who failed to embrace us milleniums ago
was now opening her arms to us & all we cld respond to
was the memory of the terrible cold, the fierce, unrelenting,
unmerciful, dehumanizing cold
& driven by that memory
we sat down at afrika's table & when we had had our fill
"we killed the host, raped the hostess & sold the children."

A HOME REMEDY U CAN BANK ON

when luv is all u want
    but fear is all u kno
when being embraced is all u crave
    but inhibitions are all u have
absolute luv is the only cure
    Spirit is the absolute healer.

PHILOSOPHY 101

no matter who u are, no matter
what u do, all of yr actions are either born of
luv, or fear.

if u move consistently in luv
u'll be one of those people otha people call lucky
the universe will be yr best-friend
& u and Spirit will always be on a first name basis.

if u move consistently in fear
u'll be one of those people otha people feel sorry for
nothing u do will ever turn out right
& u'll always be looking for someone else to blame.

CHOOSE

to live
in luv
or languish
in fear
just kno
that u cant do both.

THE WHY OF FIBROIDS

effete doctors claim blk women have more fibroid tumors than any
otha women on the planet. why, becuz we luv ourselves less than
any otha women on the planet. becuz we have been programmed
to hate ourselves more, than any otha women on the planet.
& we have kept that animosity flowing from mouth to mouth
womb to womb,
generation to generation.

if u were a tumor
needing a home full of fear, anger & self-hatred to grow in
wldnt u pick an unevolved blk woman?

A $64,000 QUESTION

what manner of ass is this
wld drop a bomb
on women, children & old people
just to keep an elephant off its back?

WARNING: THIS POME
MAY HAVE COLONIC PROPERTIES

let's stop claiming that slavery shit
stop talkin bout somebody else enslaved us
stop saying we were captured, robbed of our will
say instead that we did not honor our connectedness
with the invisible ones, or with each otha
& that our failure to reconnect brought about
MAAFA: the great suffering.

lets take responsibility for the actions
that got us here. if we must kno the reasons,
let us approach the invisible ones & sincerely ask for answers
& while the answers are on the way, lets look at all of our history
not just the parts that make us feel good. lets take a look at how
we forced ourselves on otha peoples,
in what we claimed was the name of goodness.
do u think there was not a single rape?
never more killing that necessary?
if we were as mighty as we believe, do we think that we were so
righteous that we conquered nations w/out hurting anyone?
it doesnt matter if the proof is on paper, or not.
we kno,
that when we truly walk with Spirit, our security is absolute
but the more we deviate, the more we leave ourselves open
for whatever wicked, this way cometh.
& thats exactly what we did.
so lets stop acting like we were victims/ cuz we've never been a
race of people that stuff just happens to.
whatever we did to bring about our own wretchedness
lets ask forgiveness from the universe,
for anything we ever collectively did
to disrupt the cosmic order.
lets ask forgiveness for any & all wrongdoings.
& then,   lets forgive...

Can Get U Killed

HAIKU'S

YOUNG LUV IN RETROPECT
(for Will Greene)

1

i was a peach &
a mango at
the same time
so pluckably sweet.

2

one sly-eyed glance was
all u had to
give & i
was yrs for lifetimes.

3

several women
away from u
i still knew
my worth in yr sight.

4

u wanted to get
high, my luv was
so pure, death
alone cld cut it.

Being A Strong Black Woman

5

what death does not mean
is that u can
leave me here
cloning u with tears.

6

when u find yr home
among the clouds
i will come
eventually.

HAIKU'S

BOSNIA

rape death camps, ten, twelve
times a day til
knocked up.
by seed that hates u.

HAITI

where is yr majik
where are the bones
feathers that
ustah have yr back.

CUBA

yielding to nothing
fearing no one
resisting
& breathing are same.

NIGERIA

abiola &
abacha drank
from the same
cup of US tea.

Being A Strong Black Woman

JAPAN

world's authority
on how to be
blown up &
put back together.

EL SALVADOR

those who did not die
appear, are here
surviving
til mayans rule again.

RUSSIA

now doing worse than
real communism ever
wld have treated them.

TUPAC

beauty & the beast
roamed in & out
beast took charge
beauty? suicide.

TRUTH

we are still going
thru the middle
passage, cept
now we've got tv.

AFRIKA

afrika is all
ways at the cross
roads/always
certain to be crossed.

GENOCIDE

kill all the blacks in
the whole world, afrika will
still flow thru yr veins

WASSUP

1.
wassup, somebody
tell me cuz i
been nursing
low, too long to kno.
2.
a dog is a man's
best friend, yo dog
lets go pee
& mark our corner.

RED WHITE & BLUE

amerika aint
the country it
ustah be
cuz, it never was.

Being A Strong Black Woman

AN OUNCE OF PREVENTION

hug & luv yr children
so they wont have to end
up on ricky lake.

NOT RACIALLY MOTIVATED

no matter what happens to people of color at the hands of wite
people too many of them always try to claim,
it wasnt racially motivated.

when the 4 aryan bushwackers beat, battered & bludgeoned
rodney king & cld be heard on their transmitters, freely
talkin bout killin niggahs
it wasnt racially motivated:

neither was slavery, the wholesale slaughter of the buffalo,
thousands of deplorable lynchings, decades of european
initiated scalpings,
jim-crow, the massacres at sand creek
& rosewood, the kkk, the politikal assassinations of jim thorpe
& muhamed ali, or the alledged poisoned kool-aid suicides
of over 900 amerikan borne afrikans in jonestown.

beings w/out souls, bombed a christian church in alabama, &
by way of the blast severed the lifelines of four little
blk girls who still played with dolls, but
it wasnt racially motivated:

neither was the brutal but not unusual beating of fanny lou, the
berlin conference, the fake-ass establishment of the bureau
of indian affairs, the trial of cinque,
tarzan, kit carson,the creation of amos & andy, the lone ranger
& tonto, cisco & poncho, the middle passage, the trail of tears,
the shooting of medgar evers, proposition 81,
the death of ron brown,
or the theft & misnaming of turtle island.

Being A Strong Black Woman

o.j. simpson's trial fueled the tabloids & tv talkshow monologues
for over 2 years. his mass-media lynching was on tv
everyday & given as much play as "as the world turns" or the
"dumb & the restless". jeffery dahmer ate 17 people, most of
them blk & his trial didnt receive any
of the notoriety o.j.'s did.
but, it wasnt racially motivated:

neither was the killing of alfredo teo by sheinbein, the bombing of
the blk wall st. in OK & MOVE in phila., the arrest
& incarceration of the scottsboro boys, the tuskegee experiment,
the sterilization of young blk & native amerikan girls in the '70's,
the birth of a nation, little big man, gone with the wind, or dances
with wolves.

a frustrated wite cop in ny, troubled by his innate impotence, used
a plunger to sodomize a young haitian man & across the country,
people immediately got the wrong idea,
it wasnt racially motivated:

neither was the invasion of grenada, the invasion of panama, the
murder of emmett til, the rapes of joann little, inez garcia
& matawaka (aka pocahontas), the railroading of marcus garvey,
the kangaroo trial of leonard peltier, or the events at wounded
knee.

a blk serviceman, who was obviously trippin on the wrong side of
reality, thought racism was over, & went to a party with his wite
friends & when the party got dull, they
doused him with gasoline,
 lit him up, burned him alive, &
cut off his head. the news sd they had a little too much to drink,
but that the incident was not racially motivated:

Can Get U Killed

neither was the entrapment of marion barry, the introduction of
whiskey to the native amerikans, the dispersal of crack thruout
the blk communities,
the destruction of the blk panther party,
the attempted destruction of AIM,
the formation of concentration reservations, the spectacle of
anita & clarence, the death of cosby's son, the firing of
dr. welsing from howard university,cointelpro, or the recent
attacks on blk scholarship
by leftkowitz, schlesinger & the please dont
bust our illusion posse.

nothing the wite man has ever done has been racially
motivated, including the annihilation of the native amerikans
in north, central & south amerika & the carribean,
the complete extermination of the tasmanians,
the continuous rape & pillaging of afrika, the opium attacks
on china,
the unsuccessful strangulation of cuba, the racial hierarchy
that emerged in india, the atomic bombing of hiroshima &
nagasaki,
the decimation of the aborigines in australia, or the undeclared
coflicts
in korea, vietnam, & iraq.

no matter what happens to people of color at the hands of
wite people too many of them will claim it was not racially
motivated. so what are they trying to tell us
that they're just like that?

Being A Strong Black Woman

A NOWTIME REVELATION

dont starve yr today
with intentions of feasting tomorrow.
the fruit u are holding in yr hand
is all there is
not the seed it was
or the dust it will become.

DID JIMMY KNO MUSIK?
(for Jimmy "Black Fire" Gray)

jimmy knew musik like langston knew rivers,
like afrikans knew hambone, like sitting bull knew victory
like david walker knew kujichaguila
like james cameron knew lynching, like bessie knew the blues.

jimmy knew musik like cab knew clean, like ethel knew waters,
like castro knew change, like the nicholas bros knew dance,
like the zoot-suit knew cool,
like jack johnson knew the ole one, two
like garvey knew the u.n.i.a.

jimmy knew musik like claude mckay knew fighting back
like diz knew beebop, like monk knew ebonyivory,
like zora knew mules & men, like fanny lou knew pain,
like elijah knew blue-eyed devils. like aretha knew respect.

jimmy knew musik like van sertima knows mexico, like dr. ben
knows egypt, like michael jordan knows basketball, like oprah
knows money, like marion berry knows entrapment,
like pacifica knows musik.

jimmy knew musik like langston knew ancient dusky rivers
& like langston his soul has grown deep like
the musik, the musik, the musik...

Being A Strong Black Woman

A QUALITY CONTROL CHECKLIST
FOR POETS CONSIDERING OPEN - MIKE

are yr pomes arrogant
do they think they bloomed into existence w/out any cultural
antecedents whatsoever. do they claim originality in a zone
unknown to thousands of years of blk literature. now that u've
been writing for 6 mths do yr pomes show up at readings anxious
to be heard yet deaf dumb and blind to the words of othas. do they
realize that they're part of a grand continuum or like cheese do
they think they stand alone.

are yr pomes incestuous. do they do it to each otha behind yr
back. are they matin & creating children who dont have enuff
sense not to look exactly alike.

are yr pomes ignorant. are they repositiories of stuff u made up,
or are they the end result of the books u constantly read about
black people, about the world, and about how othas experience
that world. do yr pomes make sense, or do they try to be abstract,
loaded down with words that all came staggering out of roget's
thesaurus for people who wanna sound deep.

are yr pomes for the people or are they for otha poets who just
wanna play mirror games with each otha. can yr pomes exist on
their own or do they need drama & musik to pull them up outa the
abyss of mediocrity. are u the new puba of ebonics or the last don
of caucasionics.

do yr pomes need a doctor or an undertaker. do they stumble from
one workshop to another, discoverin multiple personalities, that
when combined, still aint got nothin to say. when u share them
wif family & friends do they just smile & say, "wow...did u write
that."

Can Get U Killed

do yr pomes have yeast. are they itching to be re-written,
aching to be restructured. dyin for some ointment that will ease
the discomfort of having been written in a hurry & then
bragged about. are yr pomes circumcized.
do they need to be. can u guarantee that yr sense of literary
hygiene is acute enuff to keep us from being infected with
intellectual syphillis.

are yr pomes obsessed with one theme. are they suffering from
an alphabetic deficiency, got a bad case of iiiiiiiii. do yr pomes
show an awareness of otha life-forms. can they survive in a
space outside of yr head. do yr pomes kno they have otha rela-
tives, sired by otha writers in otha languages in otha lands. are
they wanna-be literature, one step away from bein a diary en-
try, no steps away from bein so esoteric we havta
be buddhists monks to understand. if yr pomes are found a
hundred years from now, will they be relevant to a surviving
people as inspiration or rough toilet paper.

are yr pomes drug-free. are they hooked on crack, an
occasional review, loveboat, an honorable mention. do they
trip all over themselves, tryin to slam when there's no contest.
do they tiptoe around the hood/perpetratin, imitatin & rhythm
fakin. are they inundated with profanity to disguise their lack
of profoundity. are they addicted to burnt-out meters that must
be screamed out aloud, becuz they go limp dick on paper.

do yr pomes covet they neighbor's pomes. do they wish they
were filled with words that implode & explode like sonia's. do
they spend most of their time bad-moufin othas cuz they dont
want anybody to see how naked they really are. do they flirt
with style after style, technique after technique, in hopes of

Being A Strong Black Woman

finessing their way into meaning something more than their unevolved creator is capable of imagining.

are yr pomes picked on by otha pomes becuz they have no publisher. do they come home day after day, with torn images & bloody tones from where they showed up at a reading & got punked & chased home by talent & political significance.

are yr pomes superficial. when we turn them sideways do they disappear. are they chameleons. when bloods are not around do they sound pastel instead of bright redddd. can they be called bewitching by robert haas, or bullshit by baraka. do they secretly wish they were wite & widely read or can they live with bein blk, excellent & never heard of.

are yr pomes worth the time it takes to read them. do they justify their existence by makin us FEEEEL the good, the bad & the just is. do we get excited when we see yr pomes on the printed page. do we get mad, or get glad. when we stray away from our natural selves, do yr pomes bring us back or take us further out. can they conjure. invoke in us the hunger & passion of great sex, the comedy of under-sex, or the tragedy of no sex! do yr pomes liberate anything. i dont mean do they steal, i mean do they free-up the history of ourstory. are they state-of-the-art weapons against wite supremacy. do they reveal enemies. do they unchain melodies. do they dissolve prison bars. do they rescue political prisoners. do they smoke dictators, or emasculate ebony haters. do they reflect the truth about our sun starved existence in this ice-filled reality. can they offer one useful suggestion as to how we can melt down just one new-age glacial elmina & return ourselves to solar greatness.

if your pomes dont take us to, can they at least point us towards the Promised Land. can they heal the sick & empower the poor. when verification is impossible, do yr pomes still insist upon tellin the truth. in that blessed space between the ears, do yr pomes plant subliminal suggestions that can usher us into a collective return to grace.

are yr pomes warriors or do they think they're lovers. are they engineers or just consumers. do they inform, conform or deform. in the presence of enemies do yr pomes castrate or masturbate. when the vampire fangs of this nation are baring down upon us, will yr pomes hyponotize us into removing our ankhs & offering up our jugulars, or will they whip some sunlight on that majiddy & overexpose him for the no saxophone playing MF he really is.

do yr pomes have balls. do they speak up for themselves & for us. do they imitate the lastest top-40 lyrics. can yr pomes stand to be laughted at. can they take rejection. are yr pomes, hos, ready to be revised at the behest of anybody offerin a dollar's worth of "well, we think it wld sound better like this". do they wanna be read so badly, they'd strip themselves of melanin & meanin just to receive an insufficent advance from a publisher whose ancestors were part-owners of the amistad.

are yr pomes poison darts. are they personal assassins. do u send them out to kill people who dont agree wif u, people who wont go to bed wif u, people who did go to bed wif u. do u hunt & kill wif viscious verbs & caustic nouns daily sharpened on the stone of pain u carry in yr heart for "whatever". do yr pomes go around avenging shit/not slavery or apartheid, but stuff people did to u while going thru the natural process of living their lives. when yr pomes are at their strongest,

Being A Strong Black Woman

absolutely, no-nonsense best, do they try to take us down the
dirty-dealing yellow brick road, or do they take us straight to the
great oz, and pushing aside the redwhite&blue curtain, show us
that the soundz we hear are not bill
blowing his horn but monica blowing bill.

do yr pomes transcribe for the ancestors/do they decode for us the
language of the Great Spirit.
are they wholistic, do they offer us the 411 on mind, body &
spirit. do they turn introspection into acts of luv. do they help us
see ourselves within the completeness of our own divinity. do
they help ease the pain & break the cocoon's membrane so we can
become bad, blk brazen butterflies. do yr pomes invite change.
do they coax us like babies takin first steps, into letting go of the
table, & believing we can stand on our own. do yr pomes separate
the wheat from the chaff or do they tell us its all cereal, just eat it,
its all good.

when u're makin pomes, are u makin luv or screwin. are u
consciously creating a loving being that will improve the quality
of our lives, or are u just using our eyes for condoms, where u
just dump yr seed/never looking back or caring about the effect.

yr pomes are yr children. the Most High allows u to create them
so that u too may enjoy the majestik & unparalleled splendor of
being a GOD. since yr pomes are yr children, dontchu want them
to be born with all their parts. dontchu want to see them properly
fed & nurtured. dontchu want to see them go out into the world
reflecting the burning brilliance of briteness that characterizes the
afrikan literary tradition. & before u send them out for the world
to critique, shldnt u at least bathe them, change their diapers and
wipe the snot from their noses before u go haulin them off to be
christened at an open mic?

Can Get U Killed